SALTLESS
LOW SALT COOKING

FRESH
FAST
EASY

COOKBOOK: LOW SALT RECIPES
LOW SODIUM HOME COOKING

HARPER FULLERTON
UNITED KINGDOM

Copyright

Copyright© Saltless Low Salt Cooking. Fresh Fast Easy. ISBN9780992811464
All rights reserved. No reproduction, copy or transmission of this Publication may be made without written permission from the author. No paragraph of this publication may be reproduced, copied or transmitted. Save with written permission or in accordance with provisions of the Copyright, Designs and Patents Act 1988, or under the terms of any license permitting limited copying, issued by the Copyright Licensing Agency, The Author has asserted his right to be identified as the author of this work in accordance with the Copyright, Design and Patents Act 1988
*Content Protected by DMCA FORCE Anti Piracy Protection. Any infringement will be detected and take down notice will be enforced.www.dmcaforce.com is the authorised DMCA Agent for this copyright holder.
Saltless Low Salt Cooking. Comfort Cooking is published by Harper Fullerton, Unted Kingdom. Disclaimer: Neither the Author of Publisher aim to give professional advice to the individual reader. The suggestions in this book are based on the experience of the Author only and are not intended to replace consultation with a doctor and/or dietician where health matters are concerned. Meniere's disease requires medical supervision as do all other health issues. Neither the Author or Publisher shall be responsible or liable for any injury, damage, loss arising from information or suggestions in this book as the opinions expressed are entirely derived from the Author's personal experience and the book expresses and represents the personal view of the Author. Every effort has been made to provide accurate website addresses and complete information at the date of publication, however exact measurements and cooking times are dependent on the quality of ingredients, the varying temperatures of kitchen equipment, therefore the readers commonsense is the best guide to compensate for such variables. The Author and the Publisher take no responsibility for individual health issues or specific allergies or allergy, known or otherwise, that needs specific medical supervision, or any adverse reaction to any ingredient specified, or adverse reactions to the recipes contained in this book. The recipes are chosen by the experience of the Author and are not advocated as a cure for Meniere's disease, but are based on the Author's personal experience and represents the Authors personal views on healthy eating as part of an overall plan to improve health, as experienced by the Author only. The recipes in this book and advice given are published for general interest for the reader only and are not intended to take the place of medical guidelines and recommendations by medical professionals.

CONTENTS

IN THE FAMILY	7
TEN LOW SALT COOKING TIPS	9
THE SALTLESS HOME DAIRY	15
Mozzarella Cheese	16
Ricotta Cheese	20
Crème Fraiche	23
COOKING BASICS	25
Tomato Salsa	26
Mango Salsa	28
Dukkah	30
Orange Oil	32
Prawn Oil	32
French Blend	34
Spice Island Blend	36
Moroccan Blend	37
Chicken Herbs	38
Fish Herbs	39
Pork Herbs	40
Fine Herbs	41
Bouquet Garni	42
Italian	43
Seasoning	43
INGREDIENT KNOW HOW	45
BREAKFAST	49
Angel In The Morning	50
Very Berry Smoothie	52
Banana Apple Smoothie	55

Raw Energy Juice	56
Buttermilk Pancakes	58
Breakfast Compote	60
Noah's Pancakes	62
Italian Sausages	64
Baked Beans	66
Toasted Muesli	68
Swiss Muesli	70
Fruit Muesli	72
Our Most Secret Muesli	74
Baked Granola	76
SOUPS AND STOCKS	79
Chicken Stock Without Salt	80
Beef Stock	82
Potassium Rich Vegetable Stock	84
Tomato And Saffron Soup	86
Leek And Potato Soup	88
Mushroom Soup	90
Spinach And Ginger Soup	92
Chicken Chowder	94
Pasta Soup	96
Gazpacho Soup	98
Celery Soup	102
Noah's Two Of Everything Soup	104
Soup Au Pistou	106
Eve's Chicken Broth	108
Pumpkin And Coconut Soup	110
SALSAS VEGETABLES AND SALADS	113
Herbalicious Salad	114

Avocado Dressing	116
Slow Roasted Tomatoes	118
Onion Jam	120
Avocado Salsa	122
Orange Salad	124
Avocado And Citrus Salad	126
Marinated Bean Salad	128
Mediterranean Vegetables	130
Tomato And Mint Salad	132
Roasted Red Peppers	134
Zucchini Fritters	136
Spinach Tart	138
Bus Stop Potatoes	142
Irish Potato Cake	144
Hot Potato Wedges	146
Roasted Beetroot Salad	148
Beetroot And Orange Salad	150
Best Potato Salad Ever	152
Pumpkin Salad	154
Roasted Eggplant Salad	157
Lemon Garlic Mushrooms	160
Mint Orzo Salad	162
Evergreen Café's	164
Hummus Salad	164
Tabbouleh Salad	166
Glossary	171

ALL
IN THE FAMILY

Saltless is for people who love good food and love cooking. And for those who realize that good food and good heath are compatible. Salt is hard to give up because it's a vehicle for flavor. Low salt diets often fail because just taking salt out of dishes makes the food tasteless. Boring food puts your taste buds to sleep. Eating should be a pleasure not taken as a spoonful of medicine. That's why Saltless is all about recipes that are not only low in salt, but really delicious in flavor.

Recent research shows, that anxiety from counting salt grams, increases the body's craving for salty foods. In fact, stress actually makes your body retain salt. Dr. Gregory Harshfield of Georgia Health Sciences University says, "Every time a person is stressed, they hold onto as much salt as you get when you eat a small order of French fries. And this can occur many times over the course of a day". In Saltless you'll find specific details on sodium content which relieves you of the anxiety of counting salt. We have made the counting salt grams our job so you can get on with the love of preparing delicious quick and easy low salt meals.

The question is can "lack" of salt coexist with delicious flavors? Yes it can. By adapting and testing new versions of recipes you can now change the salt habit of a lifetime. We know that eating tasty, gutsy food without salt, is truly one of life's great pleasures.

TEN LOW SALT COOKING TIPS

Cooking is a creative process and ingredients are interchangeable. If you don't have a specific ingredient, use the glossary in this book to find a substitute. When you do this, you'll create a signature dish of your own.

You can use the recipes in this book to whip up a meal with a minimum of fuss. By using fresh foods, preferably organic, you can cook dishes that taste great without salt. So, as much as possible, eat what is in season. Grow your own herbs. Use the freshest spices. Shop in local markets for the seasonal produce.

1. Use herbs and spices instead of salt.
2. Marinades and sauces don't have to include salt, soy sauce, barbecue sauce, tamari or fish sauce. Leave them out.
3. Let stocks, soups and stews cook slowly or on simmer to enhance flavor.
4. Cook stews and casseroles the day before and reheat the next day to increase flavor intensity.
5. Use stocks or wine instead of water in casseroles, soups and braised dishes.
6. Cook grains like rice and beans in stock; add herbs, garlic, and onions for a rich flavor.
7. Defat pan juices which are left after cooking. Then simply add wine or water to deglaze the frying pan on low heat. Use these juices as a flavorful sauce.
8. Make sauces from reduced meat or vegetable stocks. Add fresh herbs, season with pepper and thicken with corn flour.
9. Cook with condiments like homemade no salt added chutneys and preserves to give a glaze to roasted meats, grilled or barbecued food.
10. Don't throw out your favorite old recipes. Use the sections in this book to substitute other ingredients for salt and enjoy your familiar flavors.

THE HEALTHY PANTRY

30 LOW SALT ITEMS TO STOCK YOUR FRIDGE, FREEZER OR PANTRY

1. Homemade no salt chicken stock, meat and vegetable stock
2. Dairy: yogurt, butter, eggs
3. No salt homemade mozzarella, ricotta cheese, mascarpone, crème fraiche
4. Fresh herbs. (Grow in containers or in the garden)
5. Rice, pasta of all shapes
6. Beans, lentils and dried legumes, grains
7. Oil for cooking: olive oil
8. Oil for flavor: cold-pressed walnut, extra virgin olive oil, hazelnut, sesame
9. Tomato paste, tomato puree, tinned tomatoes
10. Vinegars: red, white, balsamic, herb infused

11. Onions, shallots, green onions, garlic, ginger
12. Lemons, limes, oranges
13. Long life vegetables: pumpkin, potatoes
14. Whole grain bread
15. Organic unbleached white flour
16. Low sodium baking powder
17. Nuts: hazelnuts, almonds.
18. Rolled oats
19. Black, white, green and dried peppercorns
20. Mushrooms: Porcini, button, brown, Portobello
21. Homemade no salt tomato sauce, barbecue sauce, chutneys
22. Wines: red and white
23. Salt free corn chips and crackers
24. Grains, wheat, couscous
25. Frozen berries: strawberries, blueberries, raspberries, and blackberries
26. Frozen organic chicken, organic steak, wild caught salmon fillets, wild caught white fish
27. Seasonal vegetables to keep in the fridge: carrots, lettuces, rocket leaves, baby spinach, celery and beetroot
28. In the freezer: no salt pizza bases
29. Exotic ingredients: quince paste, vanilla bean
30. Vegetables: peas, soya beans, green beans

THE SALTLESS HOME DAIRY

Mozzarella Cheese

One slice of bought whole milk mozzarella, can contain 178mg of sodium. One slice of saltless home made mozzarella, contains 5mg. Here is a recipe for homemade no salt mozzarella. You can make this recipe in 30 minutes. Less than the time it takes to go to the supermarket.

Makes: about 500g

Ingredients

4.5 liters of whole milk
1 1/2 tsp citric acid
1/4 tablet rennet
mineral water
* Do not use junket rennet for making mozzarella, as it is not strong enough.

Method

Mix citric acid in 1 cup cold water.

Pour milk into a heavy bottomed saucepan. Stir in citric acid mixture.

Heat the milk to 32 degrees C, stirring constantly. Remove from heat. Dissolve rennet tablet in 1/4 cup cool water. Add this slowly to the milk using an up and down motion with a slotted metal spoon. Cover with a lid. Let stand for 5 minutes. Remove lid and check the curd. It should resemble custard when pressed lightly with your finger.

Take a metal knife or spatula. Slice across the surface of the curd cutting the curd into 3cm squares. Return the saucepan to the heat and heat the curd to 40 degrees C, while slowly stirring the curd with your spoon. Remove from heat and stir for 2-5 minutes. The more you stir the firmer the mozzarella will be. Pour into a sieve or colander. The curds will drain off from the whey (the liquid). Pour curds into a microwavable bowl. Tip bowl to drain off whey. Microwave on high for 1 minute. Drain off the whey again. Microwave again for 30 seconds. Remove from bowl and place curds on a workbench. Knead, as you would bread dough, turning the cheese and folding the cheese over. Keep kneading until the cheese turns glossy. If cheese doesn't hold together, microwave for another 30 seconds on high.

Cheese is ready when it is so elastic that you can stretch it into a long strand.

Form the cheese into a loaf shape or a ball. You can plait the cheese also. Then fill a bowl with cool water and submerge the cheese for 15 minutes. This will help the cheese keep its shape and maintain a silky texture.

Cheese keeps in the fridge in a covered container for up to 2 weeks. You can also wrap the cheese tightly in cling film and freeze it.

Hot Water Bath Directions

If you don't have a microwave you can create mozzarella by using the following method. Follow cheese-making steps in the recipe up to the microwave instructions. Instead of using the microwave, heat water in a heavy saucepan to 82 degrees C. Spoon the curds into a colander or sieve, folding the curds over gently as you drain off the whey. Dip the colander into the hot water several times. Take a spoon and fold the curds until they become elastic and pliable. Remove the curds, stretch and pull. If it does not stretch easily, return to the hot water bath in the colander and repeat the process. Then continue kneading cheese until it is pliable like long elastic. Submerge in water for 15 minutes. Drain. Store covered in the fridge as directed.

Ricotta Cheese

Homemade ricotta cheese is as cheap to make as the cost of a liter of milk. Homemade ricotta makes a great base for ravioli fillings and lasagna. You can serve with freshly sliced fruit: peaches, nectarines and berries. Or with stewed stone fruit: apricots, plums or fresh figs served with a drizzle of honey.

Makes: 2 cups
Cooking time: 30 minutes

Ingredients

8 cups whole milk

1 cup plain whole milk yogurt

1/2 cup heavy cream (optional for richer cheese)

2 tsp white wine vinegar or lemon juice

Method

Heat milk, yogurt and cream (if using) and vinegar in a heavy-bottomed saucepan.

Bring to boil on medium heat. Turn heat to low and boil very gently for 2 minutes, or until milk is curdled. Remove from heat. Line a sieve or colander with 2 layers of clean cheesecloth or fine washed muslin. Set the colander into a deep bowl. Pour the milk mixture into the lined colander or sieve. Drain for 15 minutes. Pull sides of the cloth together and squeeze the curds gently to remove the whey (liquid). Remove strained curds from cloth and serve. You can store the ricotta cheese, in a covered container in the fridge for up to 3 days.

Crème Fraiche

Naturally soured fresh cream you can flavor with lemon zest, vanilla, or spices and use on top of fresh fruit for dessert.

Method

Stir 2 parts of fresh double cream with 1 part buttermilk, sour cream or yogurt (with live cultures). Stir over low heat until just warm. Allow to sit at room temperature for 6-8 hours. Stir and chill. Store covered in the fridge. Keeps for up to 3 weeks.

COOKING BASICS

Tomato Salsa

Per Serving: Sodium 8mg

Ingredients

6 medium tomatoes

2 spring onions

30 ml (2 tbsp) lemon juice

1 tbsp parsley, chopped

10 cm length cucumber, diced

2 tbsp coriander

Chopped pepper

Method

Skin and seed tomatoes. Dice. Mix all ingredients together and chill 1-2 hours.

Serve with toasted pita bread chips.

Per Serve: Fat 0.3g Cholesterol 0mg Sodium 8mg Potassium 317mg Carbohydrates 5.3g Fiber 1.7g Sugars 3.4g Protein 1.3g

Health Benefits Of Cucumber:
Rehydrates body and helps eliminate toxins. Good source of B vitamins for a quick-pick–me-up.

Mango Salsa

Per Serving: Sodium Free

Ingredients

2 cups mango, cubed
1 onion, chopped
3 tbsp onion, chopped
3 tbsp oil
1 tbsp water
Mint leaves or coriander leaves
Lime juice

Method

Place mango in a mixing bowl. Combine onion, oil and water in a saucepan. Cover and simmer on low heat for 10 minutes. Add mango. Add 1 tbsp fresh mint or coriander leaves. Stir in lime juice.

**Per serve | Fat 3.5g | Cholesterol 0mg |
Sodium 0mg | Potassium 34mg | Carbohydrates 2.2g | Fiber 0.5g | Sugars 1.0g | Protein 0.2g |**

Health Benefits Of Mango:
Boost the immune system with generous levels of vitamin C, vitamin A and 25 kinds of carotenoids.

Dukkah

Per Serving: Sodium 2mg

Ingredients

25g hazelnuts

25g almonds

1 tbsp smoked paprika

1 tbsp ground black pepper

3 tsp coriander seeds, roasted

2 tbsp thyme leaves

2 tsp garlic powder

Method

Roast nuts for 7-10 minutes. Put spices on a paper-lined baking sheet. Roast for 10 minutes, stirring frequently. Cool. Finely chop all in blender. Use as a healthy dip with yogurt; add to cooked vegetables; sprinkle over salad; coat potatoes before roasting; rub over meat or chicken before grilling or toss in cooked chickpeas for a salad.

Per Serve | Fat 4.9g | Cholesterol 0mg | Sodium 2mg | Potassium 118mg | Carbohydrates 4.2g | Fiber 2.1g | Sugars 0.7g | Protein 2.0g |

Health Benefits Of Hazelnuts:
Rich in vitamin B complex. Helps the nervous system function and helps with stress, anxiety and depression.

Orange Oil

Combine 500ml strained orange juice and 50ml strained lemon juice into a saucepan. Reduce over low medium heat until syrup-like. Cool to room temperature then whisk in an equal quantity of olive oil. Store in clean bottles. Use to drizzle over grilled fish, potatoes, salads and steamed vegetables, such as asparagus and broccoli.

Prawn Oil

Take shells from prawns you peeled. Heat light olive oil in a frying pan. Add prawn heads and tails. Fry on low heat until prawns turn pink. Cook a further 20 minutes. Cool. Strain through kitchen paper. Discard shells. Pour oil into a clean bottle. Store in the fridge. Use when grilling fish or add with lime juice and black pepper to make a dressing for seafood salad or Asian noodle salad.

French Blend

Per Serving: Sodium 2mg

Makes: 1/3 cup

Ingredients

2 tbsp dried dill

2 tbsp dried chives

1 tbsp dried oregano

2 tsp celery seeds

1/2 tsp ground black pepper

Method

Place ingredients into a blender. Process untill the herbs are well mixed together.

Per Serve | Total Fat 0.2g | Cholesterol 0mg | Sodium 2mg | Potassium 37mg | Carbohydrates 0.9g | Protein 0.3g |

Spice Island Blend

Per Serving: Sodium 2mg

Makes: 1/3 cup

Ingredients

1 tbsp ground cloves
1 tbsp cracked black pepper
1 tbsp crushed coriander seeds
1/2 tsp garlic powder

Method

Mix together and store in a cool place.

Per Serve | Fat 0.1g | Cholesterol 0mg | Sodium 2mg | Potassium 17mg | Carbohydrates 0.9g | Protein 0.1g |

Moroccan Blend

Per Serving: Sodium 2mg

Ingredients

3 tbsp ground cinnamon

1 1/2 tbsp ground black pepper

1 1/2 tbsp ground white pepper

2 1/2 tsp ground nutmeg

2 1/2 tsp ground cloves

2 1/2 tsp ground cardamom

Method

Mix together and store in a cool place.

Per Serve | Fat 0.1g | Cholesterol 0mg | Sodium 2mg |
| Potassium 17mg | Carbohydrates 0.9g | Protein 0.1g |

Chicken Herbs

Per Serving: Sodium 2mg

Ingredients

1 tbsp dried marjoram

2 tbsp dried tarragon

1 tbsp dried basil

1 tbsp dried rosemary

1 tsp paprika

Mix well and store in a jar.

Per Serve | Fat 0.1g | Cholesterol 0mg | Sodium 2mg | Potassium 17mg | Carbohydrates 0.9g | Protein 0.1g |

Fish Herbs

Per Serving: Sodium 2mg

Ingredients

3 tbsp dill

2 tbsp dried basil

1 tbsp dried tarragon

1 tbsp lemon thyme

1 tbsp dried parsley

1 tbsp dried chervil

Mix well and store in a jar.

Per Serve | Fat 0.1g | Cholesterol 0mg | Sodium 2mg | Potassium 17mg | Carbohydrates 0.9g | Protein 0.1g |

Pork Herbs

Per Serving: Sodium 2mg

Ingredients

3 tbsp ground coriander

2 tbsp ground cumin

1 tbsp ground ginger

2 tbsp dried sage

1 tbsp dried thyme

Mix well and store in a jar.

Per Serve | Fat 0.1g | Cholesterol 0mg | Sodium 2mg | Potassium 17mg | Carbohydrates 0.9g
Protein 0.1g

Fine Herbs

Per Serving: Sodium 2mg

Ingredients

2 tbsp dried chervil

2 tbsp dried chives

2 tbsp dried tarragon

2 tbsp dried parsley

Mix well and store in a jar.

Per Serve | Fat 0.1g | Cholesterol 0mg | Sodium 2mg | Potassium 17mg | Carbohydrates 0.9g | Protein 0.1g |

Bouquet Garni

Per Serving: Sodium 2mg

Ingredients

1/4 cup dried parsley leaves
4 bay leaves crumbled
2 tbsp dried thyme
2 tbsp dried marjoram

Method

Mix herbs together. Place 1 teaspoon in a small muslin bag or 6 cm square of cheesecloth doubled. Tie bag or gather up the corners and tie with kitchen string. Use in soups, stews and stocks.

Per Serve | Fat 0.1g | Cholesterol 0mg | Sodium 2mg | Potassium 17mg | Carbohydrates 0.9g | Protein 0.1g |

Italian Seasoning

Use on pizzas, pasta, herb bread, or any dish that needs Italian flavor.

Per Serving: Sodium 2mg

Ingredients

1/2 cup dried oregano

1/2 cup dried basil

1/4 cup dried parsley

1 tbsp fennel seeds, crushed

2 tbsp dried sage

1 tbsp red pepper flakes

Mix well and store in a jar.

Per Serve | Fat 0.1g | Cholesterol 0mg | Sodium 2mg | Potassium 17mg | Carbohydrates 0.9g | Protein 0.1g |

SALT SUBSTITUTES

The new salt is a garden of herbs.

Think of fresh herbs as 'the new salt'. There is an old Chinese saying, if you want to be happy all your life, plant a garden. I would add to that, plant a herb garden. Just a couple of pots or a planter box of herbs will make everything you cook taste so much better. Just a teaspoon of herbs can make food taste fresh and enlivened, giving depth and richness to stews, soups, casseroles and sauces. Seriously, there is nothing as wonderful as the scent of fresh herbs. You can put the herbs in a shaker and use them at the table instead of salt. Use as a rub for meats and chicken. Add herbs to cooked vegetables. Add to sour cream for baked potatoes. Add to yogurt or soft cheeses for a tasty dip or dressing.

Rosemary, sage, oregano and marjoram are easy to grow. If they have enough sun, they will grow on a windowsill for months and you can use them everyday. When you trim them, they will keep growing until late season. You can use fresh herbs from your garden or bought from the store and then dry them in a low oven turned off, overnight. Fill your pantry jars and tins with herb seasonings and add zest to everything you cook. Herb blends enhance foods such as fish, chicken, beef and vegetables. Piquant blends such as dill, savory, thyme and garlic can help you eliminate salt without loss or flavor or taste. Here are easy to make blends.

INGREDIENT KNOW HOW

Follow your instincts. Substitute one ingredient for another. Use other ingredients on hand, when you don't have exactly the right ingredients. The dish will be slightly different but still taste good. For example, if you don't have spinach, use rocket. If you don't have beans, use asparagus. If you don't have shallots, use red onion.

Basil goes with: Eggplants, Tomatoes, Olive oil, Lamb, Potatoes, Pine Nuts, Walnuts, Zucchini, Capsicum, Fish, Prawns, Pasta.

Bay leaves go with: Stocks, Soups, Dried beans, Lentils, Broad beans, Pork, Sweet peppers, Veal, Potatoes, Garlic, Onions, Milk

Coriander seeds go with: Beef, Lamb, Lentils, Mushrooms, Chickpeas, Eggplants, Chicken, Hazelnuts.

Chives go with: Chicken, Eggs, Fish, Potatoes, Cucumber, Celery, Beetroot, Butter, Eggs, Prawns, Fish, Beef, Shallots, Garlic, Pork,

Coriander leaves go with: Prawns, Garlic, Pork, Beef, Avocado, Fish, Ginger, Coconut, Noodles, Soup, Mint, Parsley, Chicken, Yogurt

Fennel goes with: Olive oil, Lemon juice, Pepper,

Chicken stock, Pasta, Olive oil, Tomatoes, Almonds, Walnuts, Fish, Garlic, Mushrooms, Chicken, Potatoes, Eggs, Rocket, Watercress,

Garlic goes with: Potatoes, Butter, Olive oil, Lamb, Pork, Veal, Fish, Shellfish, Basil, Rosemary, Fennel, Parsley, Spinach, Saffron, Eggs

Ginger goes with: Nutmeg, Raisins, Honey, Cinnamon, Cardamom, Almonds, Cloves, Brown sugar, Aniseed

Honey goes with: Cream, Fruit, Dried Fruit, Cardamom, Cinnamon, Nuts, Chicken, Pork, Ginger, Cloves, Dried beans

Lemons go with: Fish, Veal, Chicken, Shellfish, Fish, Cream, Eggs, Oranges, Honey, Tea, Pasta, Noodles, Rice, Raspberries, Papaya, Coriander, Cumin Seed

Mint goes with: Lamb, Potatoes, Peas, Carrots, Tea, Lime juice, Garlic, Noodles, Bean sprouts, Pork, Cucumbers, Parsley, Coriander, Cracked wheat,

Oregano goes with: Tomatoes, Eggs, Dried Beans, Rice, Grilled fish, Lamb, Sweet Corn, Sweet peppers, Chicken, Lemons, Eggplant

Parsley goes with: Butter, Garlic, Pepper, Fish, Cream, Pepper, Lemon juice, Pine Nuts, Beans, Eggs, Lentils, Chickpeas, Chives, Chervil, Tarragon, Olive oil, Pasta, Zucchini, Artichokes, Mint, Cumin, Radishes

Rosemary goes with: Lamb, Pork, Chicken, Potatoes, Bread, Olive oil, Garlic, Parsley, Onions, Tomatoes,

Yogurt, Fish, Pine nuts

Sage goes with: Butter, Pumpkin, Olive oil, Veal, Chicken, Potatoes, Sweet potato, Pasta, Duck, Lamb, Lemons, Dried beans, Peas, Onions, Leeks

Salad greens go with: Potato, Pumpkin, Eggplant, Sweet Pepper, Beetroot, Onion, Garlic, Green Beans, Dried Beans, Asparagus, Artichoke, Chickpeas, Carrot, Broccoli, Prawns, Squid, Poultry, Egg

Tarragon goes with: Chicken, Fish, Egg, Shallot, Beef, Tomatoes, Mayonnaise

Vinegar goes with: Salad Greens, Cucumber, Strawberries, Peppercorns, Herbs, Fish, Olive oil

Almonds go with: Honey, Peach, Apricot, Vanilla, Cream, Chicken

Cashews go with: Coconut milk Beans, Cauliflower, Fish, Chicken, Almond, Rice

Coconut goes with: Chicken, Fish, Beef, Rice, Turmeric, Kaffir Lime, Lemongrass

Hazelnuts go with: Almond, Pork, Duck, Cinnamon, Orange

Peanuts go with: Pork, Chicken, Beef, Cucumber, Beans

Pecans go with: Garlic, Maple Syrup, Lemon Juice, Molasses, Pine nuts, Basil, Veal, Pasta, Garlic, Rice, Salad, Lime

Pistachios go with: Rice, Yogurt, Honey, Semolina, Almond, Walnut, Pears, Garlic, Croutons, Cream

BREAKFAST

Breakfast is an important meal. Your body needs a big boost every morning to raise your metabolic rate and give you energy for the day. When you have Meniere's, the best thing you can do for yourself, is to eat breakfast before starting your day. No computer, no phone calls…until after you've eaten. Complex carbohydrates found in whole grains supply fiber and convert easily to glucose, fueling your system. Protein keeps you going.

Angel In The Morning

Smoothies boost your vitamin intake for the day.

Per Serve: Sodium 46mg

Ingredients

2 cups fresh or frozen fruit (banana, berries)
1 cup plain yogurt (to taste)
1 cup water
1-2 tbsp honey
1/2 cup fruit juice (apple, orange) or milk

Method

Place into blender. Blend until smooth.

Number of Servings 4 | Serving Size 213 g |
Per Serving | Calories 126 | Total Fat 1.0g | Cholesterol 4mg | Sodium 46mg | Potassium 415mg | Total Carbohydrates 25.8g | Sugars 17.8g | Protein 4.3g |

Good points | Low in cholesterol | Low in sodium | High in vitamin B6 |

Very Berry Smoothie

Full of antioxidants and vitamins. Whip up this smoothie and load up on nutrients.

Per Serve: Sodium 22mg

Ingredients

4 cups water or coconut water

1 cup frozen blueberries

1 banana

1 tbsp virgin coconut oil

15 almonds

1 tsp ground cinnamon

5 tbsp shredded coconut

2 tbsp honey

1 tbsp spirulina powder (optional)

Method

Place ingredients in blender. Blend for 2 minutes on high. Pour into glasses and serve.

Number of Servings 5 | Serving Size 264 g
Per Serving | Calories 130 | Total Fat 6.5g | Cholesterol 0mg | Sodium 22mg | Potassium 178m | Sugars 13.2g | Protein 2.3g |

Good points | No cholesterol | Very low in sodium | High in manganese | Very high in vitamin B6 |

Health Benefits Of Blueberries:
These berries rank 31st in antioxidant activity compared with 60 other fruits. High in vitamin A and potassium.

Banana Apple Smoothie

Per Serve: Sodium 6mg

Ingredients

1 banana
1 cup frozen raspberries
1 cup apple juice
1/2 tsp honey

Method

Place in a blender. Whizz until smooth.

Number of Servings 2 | Serving Size 310 g
Amount Per Serving | Calories 245 | Total Fat 0.5g
| Cholesterol 0mg | Sodium 6mg | Potassium 502mg
| Sugars 49.4g | Protein 1.6g |

Good points | Very low in saturated fat | No cholesterol | Very low in sodium | High in dietary fiber | High in manganese | Very high in vitamin C |

Raw Energy Juice

Per Serve: Sodium 35mg

Ingredients

1 raw beetroot, peeled, cut in chunks

2 carrots, peeled

3 apples, cored

1 stalk celery, washed

2 cm piece fresh ginger, peeled

Method

Put vegetables through a juicer. Pour into glasses and serve immediately.

Number of Servings 3 | Serving Size 230 g
Amount Per Serving | Calories 119 | Total Fat 0.4g | Cholesterol 0mg | Sodium 35mg | Potassium 364mg | Sugars 21.1g | Protein 1.0g |

Good points | Very low in saturated fat | No cholesterol | Low in sodium | High in dietary fiber | High in manganese | Very high in vitamin A | High in vitamin C |

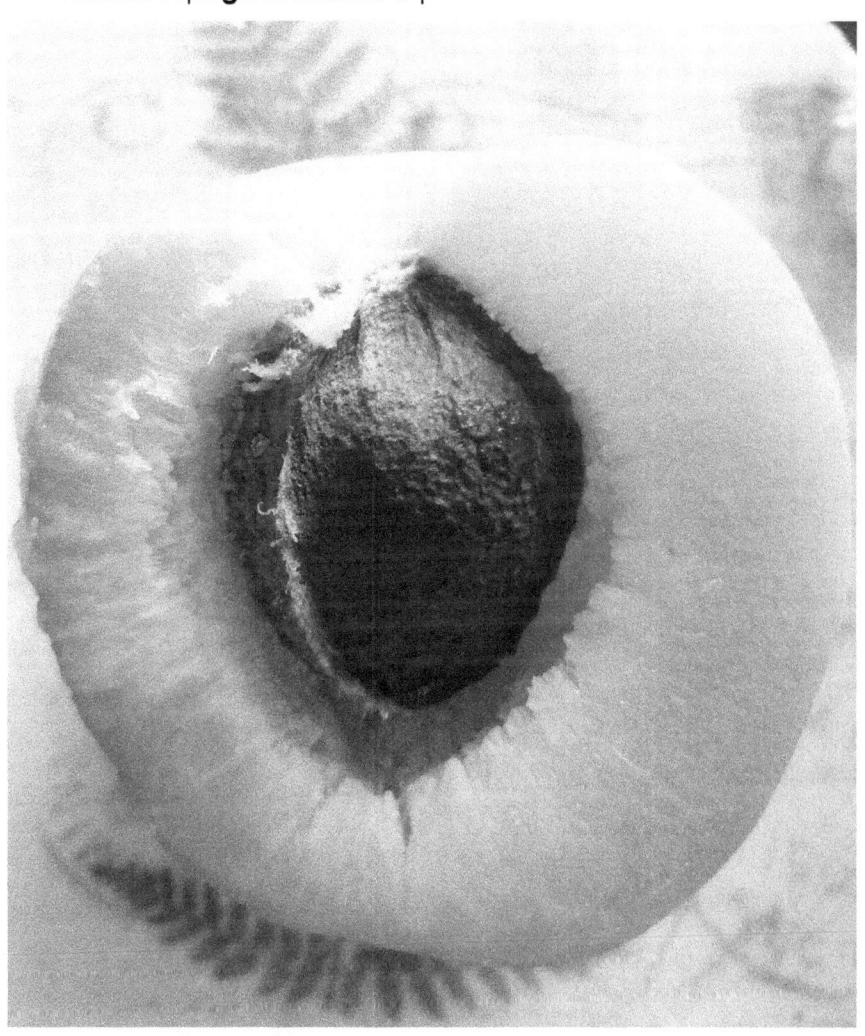

Buttermilk Pancakes

Per Serve: Sodium 57mg

250g (2 cups) organic plain flour

2 tsp baking powder

2 tbsp sugar

2 eggs lightly beaten

3 cups buttermilk

75g
Unsalted butter, melted and cooled
Unsalted butter for cooking

Method

Mix flour, baking powder and sugar together.

Whisk eggs, melted butter and buttermilk together. Stir into flour and whisk together until smooth. Heat frying pan over medium heat. Add a knob of butter. Melt butter. Spoon 1/3 cup pancake mixture for each pancake into pan. Cook until one side bubbles. Flip over. Cook for another minute until golden. Serve pancakes with stewed or fresh fruit, maple syrup and plain yogurt.

Number of Servings 16 | Serving Size 73 g
Amount Per Serving | Calories 127 | Total Fat 5.4g | Cholesterol 34mg | Sodium 57mg | Potassium 52mg | Total Carbohydrates 15.7g | Sugars 3.6g | Protein 3.8g |

Good points | Low in sodium |

Breakfast Compote

Make this up and store covered in the fridge.

Per Serve: Sodium 5mg

Ingredients

1 cup dried figs

500 ml apple juice

2 cups water

1/2 cup raw sugar

3 cinnamon sticks

10 whole cloves

10 peppercorns

4 green cardamom pods, crushed

1 vanilla bean, split in half lengthwise

Rind of 1 lemon or lime cut in thin strips

1 cup dark raisins

6 fresh pears (or apples) peeled

Method

Soak figs in water for 2 hours. Drain. Set aside. In a saucepan, combine fruit juice, water, sugar, cinnamon, peppercorns, vanilla bean, cloves and lemon rind. Simmer for 15 minutes on low heat. Add dried fruits. Simmer for a further 10 minutes. Using a slotted spoon, remove the fruits and place in a bowl. Add pears or (apples) and poach in the same saucepan for 8 minutes, until cooked but firm. Add dried fruits back to the pan. Cool to room temperature. Place in a serving bowl. Serve at room temperature or chilled, with plain yogurt.

Number of Servings 17 | Serving Size 161 g
Amount Per Serving | Calories 142 | Total Fat 0.4g | Cholesterol 0mg | Sodium 5mg | Potassium 290mg | Carbohydrates 37.1g | Sugars 27.2g | Protein 1.1g |

Good points | Very low in saturated fat | No cholesterol | Very low in sodium | High in dietary fiber | High in manganese | Very high in vitamin B6 | Very high in vitamin C |

Noah's Pancakes

Per Serve: Sodium 67mg

Ingredients

2 cups (organic) plain flour

2 eggs

2 egg yolks

2 cups milk

2 tbsp unsalted butter, melted

Method

Place all ingredients in a blender. Blend until smooth. Or place in a bowl and whisk together. Heat butter in a crepe pan or small frying pan. Add pancake batter. Roll around the pan to coat thinly. These are French crepe style (not thick). Cook on medium heat a few minutes. Flip over and cook the other side. Remove from pan. Keep warm in a low oven. Repeat until you have a stack of pancakes. Serve with your choice of maple syrup, berries, bananas, honey, or with a squeeze of lime or lemon and a little caster sugar.

Number of Servings 8 | Serving Size 111 g
Amount Per Serving | Calories 199 | Total Fat 6.7g | Cholesterol 106mg | Sodium 67mg | Potassium 89mg | Total Carbohydrates 27.1g | Sugars 2.9g | Protein 7.3g |

Good points | Low in sodium | High in selenium | High in vitamin B6 |

kitchen paper. Serve hot.

Number of Servings 6 | Serving Size 201 g
Amount Per Serving | Calories 199 | Calories from Fat 71 | Total Fat 7.9g | Cholesterol 27mg | Sodium 21mg | Potassium 763mg | Carbohydrates 29.2g | Sugars 2.2g | Protein 4.0g |

Good points | Very low in sodium | High in potassium | Very high in vitamin B6 | Very high in vitamin C |

Italian Sausages

Per Serve: Sodium 55mg

Ingredients

1 kg minced chicken/veal
1 medium onion, roughly chopped
1/2 cup flat-leaf parsley, finely chopped
2 tbsp fresh sage, finely chopped
6 cloves garlic, finely minced
1 tsp ground fennel seeds
1/2 tsp ground cloves
1 tsp ground black pepper

Method

Combine ingredients in a mixing bowl. Mix well.

Form into 6 sausages. Roll in a little flour to dust. Set aside in the fridge for 1 hour before cooking. Heat a frying pan with a little oil. Place sausages into the pan. Cook over medium heat until brown.

Number of Servings 12 | Serving Size 97 g
Amount Per Serving | Calories 135 | Total Fat 2.6g | Cholesterol 64mg | Sodium 55mg | Potassium 199mg | Total Carbohydrates 2.0g | Protein 24.5g |

Good points | Low in sodium | Low in sugar | Very high in niacin | High in phosphorus | Very high in selenium | Very high in vitamin B6 |

Health Benefits Of Parsley:
Rich in vitamin C, B12, K and A. Heals the nervous system.

Baked Beans

Per Serving: Sodium 35mg

Ingredients

1 tbsp olive oil
1 onion, finely chopped
1 clove garlic
1 tsp fresh thyme leaves, finely chopped
1/2 tsp dried oregano
400g tinned tomatoes
2 x 400g tins no salt added cannellini beans, rinsed and drained or 800g cooked dried beans
Freshly ground black pepper

Method

Heat oven to 160 C. Place oil in a casserole dish. Heat over medium heat. Add onions. Cook until transparent. Add garlic, thyme, oregano and cook for 1 minute. Add tomatoes and 1/2 cup water. Bring to boil on medium heat. Reduce heat to low and simmer 10 minutes. Remove from heat. Place lid on casserole. Bake in oven for 25 minutes. Season with pepper.

Number of Servings 6 | Amount Per Serving 222g | Calories 485 | Total Fat 3.6g | Cholesterol 0mg | Sodium 35mg | Potassium 2065mg | Carbohydrates 84.7g | Sugars 5.5g | Protein 32.2g |

Good points | Very low in saturated fat | No cholesterol | Very low in sodium | Very high in dietary fiber | High in iron | High in phosphorus | High in potassium | Very high in vitamin B6 |

Toasted Muesli

Per Serving: Sodium 5mg

Ingredients

300g (3 cups) organic rolled oats

125 ml (1/2 cup) apple juice

2 tbsp light olive oil

1/2 cup almonds (with skins on)

1 cup sunflower seeds

1/4 cup pepitas (pumpkin seeds)

1/2 cup flaked coconut

1 cup dried blueberries, cranberries, or raisins

Method

Heat oven to 160 C. Place ingredients in a bowl, except the dried berries. Spread over an oven tray in one layer. Bake 25-30 minutes, until golden brown. Turn the mixture over while baking to cook evenly. Remove from heat. Add dried fruit. Cool. Place in a covered container in the fridge. Keeps up to 1 month. To serve, place in serving bowls. Add milk, yogurt and serve with fresh berries or grated apple and a dusting of cinnamon.

Number of Servings 8 | Serving Size 97 g
Amount Per Serving | Calories 299 | Total Fat 15.6g | Cholesterol | Sodium 5mg | Potassium 302mg | Carbohydrates 33.9g | Sugars 4.7g | Protein 8.8g |

Good points | No cholesterol | Very low in sodium | Very high in manganese | High in vitamin B6 |

Swiss Muesli

Per Serving: Sodium 35mg

Ingredients

1 cup organic rolled oats
1/2 cup barley flakes
3/4 cup milk
1 apple, cored, grated with skin
1 punnet fresh blueberries (or use 1 extra apple)
1 tbsp honey
1/2 cup plain yogurt
1/4 cup almond flakes, toasted
1/2 tsp cinnamon

Method

Mix oats and barley with milk. Refrigerate overnight. Next morning add the other ingredients and serve.

Number of Servings 10 | Serving Size 96 g
Amount Per Serving | Calories 112 | Total Fat 2.5g | Cholesterol 2mg | Sodium 35mg | Potassium 130mg | Carbohydrates 19.8g | Sugars 8.3g | Protein 3.6g |

Good points | Very low in cholesterol | Low in sodium | High in manganese | Very high in vitamin B6 |

Health Benefits Of Barley:
Good source of vitamin B1, chromium, magnesium, zinc.

Fruit Muesli

Per Serving: Sodium 14mg

Ingredients

200g (2 cups) organic rolled oats

1 cup water

2 tbsp organic stabilized wheat germ

2 tbsp honey

2 tbsp toasted hazelnuts or almonds, chopped

1 apple, grated with skin on

1 cup orange, pear or apple juice

1/2 tsp cinnamon

1/2 cup yogurt

Method

Soak rolled oats in water overnight. Add yogurt, honey, wheat germ and nuts. Top with grated apple and a dusting of powdered cinnamon. Instead of apple use any fresh fruit, cut in chunks, e.g. nectarines, peaches, apricots, oranges, berries or banana.

Number of Servings 8 | Serving Size 132 g
Amount Per Serving | Calories 162
Calories from Fat 25 | Total Fat 2.8g | Cholesterol 1mg | Sodium 14mg | Potassium 241mg | Carbohydrates 29.9g | Sugars 10.8g | Protein 5.1g |

Good points | Low in saturated fat | Very low in cholesterol | Very low in sodium | Very high in manganese | Very high in vitamin B6 |

Health Benefits Of Oats:
High in fiber and a good source of essential vitamins. Contains beta glucan, which speeds up the body's response to infection and helps with faster healing.

Our Most Secret Muesli

Per Serving: Sodium 18mg

Ingredients

3 cups rolled oats

1 cup rye flakes

1 cup oat bran

1/2 cup pumpkin seeds

1/2 cup sunflower seeds

1/2 cup wheat germ

1/2 cup almonds

1/4 cup sesame seeds

1/2 cup shredded coconut

3 cups mixed dried fruits e.g. apricots, raisins,

apple, ginger

1 tsp grated nutmeg

1-2 tsp cinnamon

Method

Combine all ingredients together. Store in sealed containers in the fridge. Use as a dry muesli served with yogurt, fruit and honey. Or serve as moist muesli. For moist muesli, soak 2 cups of dry muesli in a cup of water overnight in the fridge. Mix with 1/2 cup of natural yogurt, 2 tbsp freshly chopped almonds and top with grated apple or your choice of fresh fruit.

Amount of servings 18 | Serving Size 59 g
Amount Per Serving | Calories 152 | Total Fat 7.0g | Cholesterol 0mg | Sodium 18mg | Potassium 226mg | Carbohydrates 18.7g | Sugars 3.6g | Protein 5.7g |

Good points | No cholesterol | Very low in sodium | High in dietary fiber | Very high in manganese | High in magnesium | High in phosphorus |

Health Benefits Of Rye:
Supplys high levels of iron, calcium, potassium and zinc. Helps to balance blood sugar levels.

Baked Granola

Per Serving: Sodium 3mg

Ingredients

2 cups raw organic oats
1/2 cup sunflower seeds
1 tsp ground cinnamon
3 tsp honey
100 ml mild olive oil
2 tsp pure vanilla extract
1/4 cup slivered almonds
1/4 cup pine nuts
Dried berries (blueberries, cranberries or dried cherries) to add at the end of cooking.

Method

Heat oven to 160 C. Place dry ingredients in a large bowl. Add honey, oil, vanilla and mix well. Spread onto a baking tray. Bake 10 minutes. Turn over. Bake a further 10 minutes. Remove from oven. Stir in dried berries. Cool. Place into airtight container. Keeps 2 weeks in the fridge or in freeze for up to 3 months.

Number of Servings 5 | Serving Size 105 g
Amount Per Serving | Calories 422 | Total Fat 30.6g | Cholesterol 0mg | Sodium 3mg | Potassium 253mg | Carbohydrates 33.2g | Sugars 7.4g | Protein 7.4g |

Good points | No cholesterol | Very low in sodium | High in manganese | High in vitamin B6 |

SOUPS AND STOCKS

Chicken Stock Without Salt

Per Serving: Sodium 56mg

Ingredients

6 parsley stalks, finely chopped

2 sprigs of fresh thyme, or pinch of dried thyme

1 bay leaf

6 peppercorns

1.5 liters cold water

1 whole chicken

250ml white wine or water

50g butter

2 leeks (white part only) finely chopped

1/2 carrot, finely chopped

1 stick celery, finely chopped

1 clove garlic, finely chopped
1 small onion, finely chopped

Method

Melt butter in a saucepan. Add leek, celery, carrot, garlic and onion. Cook over low heat until the vegetables become transparent and soft. Add the whole chicken, turning it in the vegetables. Add herbs and peppercorns. Add 250ml of water or wine. Place lid on the pot. Steam chicken over high heat for 5 minutes. Add the cold water and bring to a slow simmer. Simmer for 1 hour.
Cool chicken and remove meat and skin. Place bones back into the pot. Simmer for another hour. Strain bones through a fine sieve. Cool. Place in fridge overnight. Remove any fat. Store in the fridge or freezer.
Poached chicken can be used in recipes such as salads, pasta and sandwiches.

Amount of servings 8 | Serving Size 274 g
Amount Per Serving | Calories 71 | Total Fat 5.2g | Cholesterol 13mg | Sodium 56mg | Potassium 113mg | Carbohydrates 5.8g | Sugars 1.8g | Protein 0.7g |

Good points | High in iron | Very high in vitamin A | Very high in vitamin B6 | Very high in vitamin C |

Beef Stock

Per Serving: Sodium 79mg

Ingredients

1.5 kg beef marrow bones
2 large carrots
2 onions, quartered
3 stalks celery, cut in chunks
2.25 liters cold water
2 parsley stalks
1 bay leaf
8 black peppercorns
1/2 tsp dried thyme

Method

Heat oven to 230 C (450 F)

Place bones, carrot, onions and celery in a roasting pan. Place in oven and roast for 40 minutes. Remove from oven and place bones and vegetables into a large saucepan. Place 2 cups of the water in the roasting pan and cook on medium heat, stirring the brownings off the bottom. Remove from heat and pour over the bones. Add the rest of the water, parsley, peppercorns and thyme.

Bring to boil on high heat. Skim off scum and discard. Lower heat, cover pan with lid and simmer gently for 4 hours. Cool. Strain through a sieve. Place in the fridge covered overnight. Remove congealed fat. Stock is ready to use or freeze in batches for later use.

Amount of servings 15 | Serving Size 277 g
Amount Per Serving | Calories 196 | Total Fat 6.2g | Cholesterol 89mg | Sodium 79mg | Potassium 463mg | Carbohydrates 2.3g | Sugars 1.1g | Protein 30.6g |

Good points | Low in sodium | Low in sugar | Very high in iron | High in niacin | High in phosphorus | Very high in selenium | High in vitamin A | Very high in vitamin B6 | Very high in vitamin B12 | Very high in zinc |

Potassium Rich Vegetable Stock

Use as a base for soups, sauces or in stews to replace water or wine.

Per Serving: Sodium 33mg

Ingredients

1 cup onion, chopped
1 carrot, coarsely chopped
1 cup celery, coarsely chopped
1 whole head garlic, skins removed
2 strips lemon peel
2 bay leaves

2 sprigs thyme

1 tbsp oregano

5 sprigs flat-leaf parsley

10 peppercorns

1 small cinnamon stick

Olive oil

Method

Place a little olive oil in a stock pan. Heat on medium. Add vegetables. Cook for 10 minutes until the onions become transparent. Take care not to brown. Reduce heat. Cover vegetables with water. Bring to boil. Reduce heat to simmer. Cover pan and simmer for 40 minutes. Remove from heat. Cool. Strain broth through a sieve. Store in covered containers in the freezer or fridge.

Number of servings 6 | Serving Size 127g
Amount Per Serving | Calories 36 | Total Fat 0.3g | Cholesterol 0mg | Sodium 33mg | Potassium 210mg | Carbohydrates 8.4g | Sugars 2.4g | Protein 0.9g |

Good points | Low in saturated fat | No cholesterol | High in calcium | Very high in dietary fiber | Very high in iron | Very high in manganese | High in magnesium | High in potassium | Very high in vitamin A | Very high in vitamin B6 | Very high in vitamin C |

Tomato And Saffron Soup

An exotic fresh tasting soup with a deliciously complex flavor.

Per Serving: Sodium 12mg

Ingredients

1 onion, finely sliced

2 leeks, white part only, finely sliced

6 cloves garlic, crushed

8 large ripe tomatoes, chopped

1 heaped tsp saffron stamens

1 sprig fresh thyme

1 sprig fresh marjoram or oregano

500 ml chicken stock

1 tbsp tomato paste

Freshly ground black pepper

Method

Heat a little olive oil. Add onions, garlic and leeks. Cook until soft and transparent. Add tomatoes, saffron, thyme, oregano and saffron. Add chicken stock. Simmer on low heat for 20 minutes. Add tomato paste to taste. Stir. Simmer 5 minutes on low heat. Season with pepper. Cool. Place in food processor or blender and process until smooth. Reheat and serve.

Amount of servings 10 | Serving Size 181 g
Amount Per Serving | Calories 38 | Total Fat 0.3g | Cholesterol 0mg | Sodium 12mg | Potassium 310mg | Carbohydrates 8.5g | Sugars 3.9g | Protein 1.5g |

Good points | Very low in saturated fat | No cholesterol | Low in sodium | Very high in dietary fiber | Very high in iron | Very high in manganese | High in magnesium | Very high in potassium | Very high in vitamin A | Very high in vitamin B6 | Very high in vitamin C |

Leek And Potato Soup

Per Serving: Sodium 69mg

Ingredients

4 leeks (white part only)
2 large potatoes, peeled and diced
1 onion, finely chopped
50g butter
900 ml chicken stock
275 ml milk
Freshly ground white or black pepper
2 tbsp chopped parsley or chives for garnish

Method

Cut off the green top and tough outer layer of the leeks. Split the stalks and clean well to remove any earth. Cut them finely. Drain.

Place butter in a heavy saucepan. Add leeks, onion and potatoes. Stir well. Cover and cook on a low heat for 10 minutes. Add stock and milk. Stir well. Bring to a simmer. Place lid on the pan. Cook gently for about 20 minutes, stirring frequently. Remove from heat. Cool. Place in a blender and puree. Return to pan. Add freshly ground pepper. Place in a serving bowl or individual bowls. Add garnish. You can serve this soup hot or chilled. Chilled potato and leek soup is called Vichyssoise.

Amount of servings 8 | Serving Size 267 g
Amount Per Serving | Calories 133 | Total Fat 6.0g | Cholesterol 16mg | Sodium 69mg | Potassium 345mg | Carbohydrates 17.7g | Sugars 4.5g | Protein 2.9g |

Good points | Low in sodium | High in vitamin A | Very high in vitamin B6 | Very high in vitamin C |

Health Benefits Of Leeks:
Helps insomnia and anxiety. A good source of vitamin A, vitamin B6 and vitamin C. Contains antioxidant properties and protects blood vessels.

Mushroom Soup

Per Serving: Sodium 32mg

Ingredients

350g Portobello or brown mushrooms

2 large potatoes, peeled and chopped

25g unsalted butter

2 cloves garlic, finely chopped

Freshly ground black pepper

1 tsp finely chopped fresh oregano

6 cups homemade chicken stock

1/2 cup milk or thin cream

Method

Wash mushrooms. Chop. Heat butter in a large saucepan. Add garlic and mushrooms. Cook on medium heat for 10 minutes. Add potatoes, stock and oregano. Bring to the boil on medium heat. Reduce heat to low and simmer for 20 minutes. Cool to room temperature. Place soup in a blender in small batches. Place blended soup back in the saucepan. Add milk or cream very slowly while heat is on low. Do not boil. Serve in a soup tureen or in individual bowls. Garnish with parsley. Serve with toasted garlic croutons.

Amount of servings 9 | Serving Size 261 g
Amount Per Serving | Calories 69 | Total Fat 2.7g | Cholesterol 7mg | Sodium 32mg | Potassium 332mg | Carbohydrates 9.7g | Sugars 1.8g | Protein 2.5g |

Good points | Low in sodium | High in iron | High in niacin | High in pantothenic acid | High in potassium | High in riboflavin | Very high in vitamin B6 | Very high in vitamin C |

Spinach And Ginger Soup

Per Serving: Sodium 55mg

Ingredients

2 leeks, white part only, sliced

50 ml olive oil

4 cloves garlic

40g fresh ginger root, to taste

1.5 liters chicken stock

500g English spinach, washed, stalks removed
Ground black pepper to taste

Method

Place oil in a pan. Add leeks, ginger and garlic. Cook over low heat. Add stock. Simmer 10 minutes. Add spinach. Bring to the boil. Serve hot.

Amount of servings 9 | Serving Size 254 g
Amount Per Serving | Calories 87 | Total Fat 5.8g | Cholesterol 0mg | Sodium 55mg | Potassium 412mg | Carbohydrates 8.4g | Sugars 1.2g | Protein 2.4g |

Good points | No cholesterol | High in iron | Very high in manganese | High in magnesium | High in potassium | Very high in vitamin A | High in vitamin B6 | Very high in vitamin C |

Health Benefits Of Spinach:
Important for skin, hair and bone health. Provides protein, iron, calcium, magnesium and vitamin A. One of the best sources of dietary potassium.

Chicken Chowder

Per Serving: Sodium 40mg

3 tbsp unsalted butter
2 onions, finely diced
2 stalks celery, finely chopped
2 large carrots, peeled and diced
2 potatoes, peeled and diced
1/2 cooked chicken, shredded
2 bay leaves
1 sprig fresh thyme
Freshly ground pepper, preferably white
1 1/2 cups fresh or frozen corn kernels

6 cups chicken stock or water

3 tbsp cornflour, mixed with a 5 tbsp milk

3 tbsp flat-leaf parsley, chopped

Method

Heat butter in a large saucepan. Add onions and fry until transparent, about 3 minutes. Add celery and carrots. Cook until softened. Add stock, bay leaves, thyme and pepper. Cook for 25 minutes on low heat. Add corn kernels and chicken. Add cornflour paste and stir in the rest of the milk. Add to soup. Cook 4 minutes. Adjust seasoning. Add parsley. Serve hot with French bread slices: grill both sides. Rub with garlic cloves. Brush with extra virgin olive oil and serve warm.

Amount of servings 11 | Serving Size 230 g
Amount Per Serving | Calories 93 | Total Fat 3.4g | Cholesterol 8mg | Sodium 40mg | Potassium 295mg | Carbohydrates 14.9g | Sugars 2.6g | Protein 1.7g |

Good points | Low in sodium | High in dietary fiber | Very high in vitamin A | Very high in vitamin B6 | Very high in vitamin C |

Health Benefits Of Sweet Corn:
High in fiber. Protects the body from cancer and heart disease.

Pasta Soup

Per Serving: Sodium 40mg

Ingredients

1 carrot, diced
2 potatoes, diced
1 stalk celery, diced
4 large tomatoes, peeled and diced
1.5 liters chicken stock
400g tin low salt tomato puree
1 cup dried cannellini beans (cooked for 1 1/2 hours. Drain.)
200g dried small tubular pasta
2 cloves garlic, chopped
1 small piece chili
Fresh rosemary, sage, basil, finely chopped

Freshly ground black pepper
1 homemade Italian sausage
Extra virgin olive oil

Method

Heat 4 tbsp chicken stock with 2 tbsp olive oil. Add garlic and 'sweat' it for 2 minutes. Add tomatoes, potatoes, celery, carrot and stir well. Add remaining stock. Bring to boil. Simmer 20 minutes on low heat. Add cooked beans, pasta, chili, basil, rosemary and sage. Taste for seasoning. Cook a further 10 minutes. Pour into bowls. Drizzle with extra virgin olive oil and serve.

Makes 12 servings | Serving Size 276 g
Amount Per Serving | Calories 154 | Cholesterol 13mg | Sodium 40mg | Potassium 662mg | Carbohydrates 29.3g | Sugars 3.7g | Protein 7.3g |

Good points | Low in saturated fat | Low in sodium | High in dietary fiber | High in iron | High in potassium | High in thiamin | High in vitamin A | High in vitamin C |

Health Benefits Of Pasta:
Contains selenium, a mineral that protects the body from cell damage. Contains manganese to metabolize carbohydrates and regulate blood sugar. Excellent source of vitamin B9, foliate.

Gazpacho Soup

Per Serving: Sodium 59mg

Ingredients

1 kg tomatoes, peeled, seeded, finely chopped

400g tin low salt tomato puree

500 ml homemade chicken stock

2-4 cloves garlic, peeled and crushed

3 tbsp white wine vinegar

1 1/2 tbsp. olive oil

A few red pepper flakes

Fresh basil, marjoram, mint or parsley

Garnish:

1 large red capsicum

1 large green capsicum

6 slices bread, cut in cubes

1 small cucumber

1 large red onion

Olive oil to fry croutons

Black pepper, freshly ground

Method

Place tomatoes in a soup tureen. Add tomato puree, chicken stock, vinegar, olive oil and crushed garlic. Season with pepper and red pepper flakes to taste. Place in fridge.

For Garnish: chop cucumber, capsicums and onion into small cubes and place in individual bowls. Cover with plastic wrap and place in the fridge. Just before serving, heat olive oil in a frying pan and add bread. Fry to make croutons. Drain on kitchen paper. When cool place in a bowl.

Place the tureen on the table surrounded by the 4 bowls of garnishes. Serve soup and top with garnishes to taste.

Makes 8 servings | Serving Size 338 g
Amount Per Serving | Calories 112 | Total Fat 5.1g | Cholesterol 0mg | Sodium 59mg | Potassium 575mg | Carbohydrates 15.4g | Sugars 7.4g | Protein 2.8g |

Good points | No cholesterol | Low in sodium | High in dietary fiber | High in iron | High in manganese | High in potassium | Very high in vitamin A | Very high in vitamin B6 | Very high in vitamin C |

Health Benefits Of Red Capsicum:
High in vitamin A and vitamin C. Helps the absorption of iron. Contains B6 and magnesium; decreases anxiety.

Celery Soup

Per Serving: Sodium 81mg

Ingredients

350g celery stalks, chopped
2 tbsp celery leaves
120g potatoes, peeled and cut in chunks
2 leeks, white part only, washed and sliced
25g unsalted butter
580 ml chicken stock
150 ml single cream
150 ml milk
Black pepper

Method

Melt butter in a large saucepan over medium heat. Add celery, potatoes and leeks. Stir well. Cook for 10 minutes. Add stock. Bring to a simmer and reduce heat to low. Cover. Cook for 20-25 minutes. Cool. Place soup in a blender and puree. Return to pan and add milk and cream. Bring to boil on medium heat. Season with pepper. Heat though but take care not to boil.

Makes 6 servings | Serving Size 258 g
Amount Per Serving | Calories 88 | Total Fat 3.7g | Cholesterol | Sodium 81mg | Potassium 342mg | Carbohydrates 11.5g | Sugars 3.4g | Protein 2.8g |

Good points | High in calcium | High in potassium | High in vitamin A | Very high in vitamin B6 | High in vitamin C |

Noah's Two Of Everything Soup

Per Serving: Sodium 40mg

Ingredients

2 carrots, peeled, diced

2 parsnips, peeled, diced

2 onions, diced

2 cloves garlic, crushed

2 potatoes, diced

2 leeks, white part only, thinly sliced

2 celery stalks, cut thinly

2 bunches flat-leaf parsley, chopped

2 peas

2 beans

2 tbsp olive oil

Method

Heat a frying pan with oil. Fry onions and garlic for 3 minutes until tender. Add the rest of the vegetables. Cook over medium heat. Cook for 10 minutes. Add beef stock to cover the vegetables. Bring to boil. Reduce heat. Cover and simmer for 30 minutes. Remove from heat. Season with black pepper. You can serve this soup two ways. As is, with parsley to garnish. Or blend the soup with 1/2 cup light cream or 1/2 cup of milk to make a cream soup.

Makes 6 servings | Serving Size 242 g
Amount Per Serving | Calories 176 | Total Fat 5.1g | Cholesterol 0mg | Sodium 40mg | Potassium 740mg | Carbohydrates 31.2g | Sugars 7.1g | Protein 3.3g |

Good points | Low in saturated fat | No cholesterol | Low in sodium | High in dietary fiber | High in manganese | High in potassium | Very high in vitamin A | Very high in vitamin B6 | Very high in vitamin C |

Soup Au Pistou

Per Serving: Sodium 26mg

Ingredients

1 onion, chopped
3 tbsp olive oil
2 tomatoes, chopped
2 potatoes, peeled and diced
1.5 liters cold water
2 leeks, white part only, sliced
2 carrots, peeled and diced
1 cup cooked cannellini beans
250g green beans, cut into 5cm pieces
Freshly ground black pepper

Ingredients For Pistou

3 cloves garlic, peeled

1 cup loosely packed basil leaves, washed

3 tbsp extra virgin olive oil (low acid)

Method

Prepare Pistou: Place oil in a food processor or blender. Add garlic and basil leaves. Blend to a paste. Place in a serving bowl and cover. .

Prepare Soup: Sauté onion in oil until transparent. Add tomato. Sauté for 5 minutes. Add water. Bring to a simmer on medium heat. Add potato, leek, carrots and cannellini beans. Simmer for 15 minutes on low heat. Add green beans. Simmer for 5 minutes. Season with freshly ground black pepper. Place in a serving bowl. Serve a teaspoon of Pistou on top of each bowl of soup.

Makes 10 servings | Serving Size 306 g
Amount Per Serving | Calories 159 | Total Fat 4.5g | Cholesterol 0mg | Sodium 26mg | Potassium 631mg | Carbohydrates 25.2g | Sugars 3.7g | Protein 6.2g |

Good points | Low in saturated fat | No cholesterol | Very low in sodium | High in dietary fiber | High in potassium | Very high in vitamin A | Very high in vitamin B6 | Very high in vitamin C |

Eve's Chicken Broth

Per Serving: Sodium 42mg

Ingredients

1 small chicken

8 cups water

Pepper

1 onion

A few sprigs of thyme, marjoram or parsley

1 bay leaf

1 tsp lemon rind

1 tbsp uncooked rice

1 tbsp parsley, chopped

Method.

Wash chicken. Place in a large saucepan. Add water. Bring to a simmer. Add herbs and a whole onion. Bring to boil. Turn down heat. Simmer on low for 2 hours. During the last 20 minutes, add rice. Cook a further 20 minutes. Turn off heat. Cool. Strain. Flavor with pepper, lemon juice and add some chopped parsley.

Makes 8 servings | Serving Size 281 g
Amount Per Serving | Calories 94 | Total Fat 1.7g | Cholesterol 43mg | Sodium 42mg | Potassium 129mg | Carbohydrates 2.3g | Sugars 0.5g | Protein 16.3g |

Good points | Low in sodium | Low in sugar | Very high in niacin | High in phosphorus | Very high in selenium | Very high in vitamin B6 |

Pumpkin And Coconut Soup

A rich Asian flavored soup.

Per Serving: Sodium 19mg

Ingredients

500g (1lb) pumpkin, peeled and cut in cubes.
1 tbsp lime or lemon juice
1/2 cup hot water
1/2 cup onion, chopped
1 stalk lemon grass, finely chopped
2 cups thin coconut milk
1 cup thick coconut milk
1/2 cup fresh basil leaves
1 cup homemade chicken stock

Method

Place pumpkin in a bowl. Sprinkle with lime or lemon juice. Set aside. Place onions, lemon grass in food processor and blend to a paste. Place in saucepan with thin coconut milk. Bring to boil, reduce heat and simmer for 5 minutes. Add pumpkin and cook until soft and tender. Stir in thick coconut milk and basil leaves. Bring to boil. Thin the soup with chicken stock. Stir. Serve hot decorated with shredded basil leaves.

Makes 6 servings | Serving Size 242 g
Amount Per Serving | Calories 222 | Total Fat 19.4g | Cholesterol 0mg | Sodium 19mg | Potassium 442mg | Carbohydrates 13.4g | Sugars 5.9g | Protein 3.0g |

Good points | No cholesterol | Very low in sodium | High in manganese | Very high in vitamin A | Very high in vitamin B6 |

Health Benefits Of Coconut Milk:
Highly nutritious, rich in fiber, vitamins C, E, B1, B3, B5, B6, calcium and magnesium. Antibacterial compounds protect the body from infections and viruses.

SALSAS VEGETABLES AND SALADS

Herbalicious Salad

Use magical fresh herbs and greens.

Per Serving: Sodium 6mg

Ingredients

Mixed lettuce leaves (radicchio, oak leaf, baby spinach) broken into small pieces
2 tsp mint leaves
1/2 tsp sage
2 tsp dill
2 tsp tarragon
1/2 tsp marjoram
1/2 tsp oregano
2 tsp chervil
30 ml red wine or balsamic vinegar
90 ml extra virgin olive oil

Method

Combine lettuce and herbs in a salad bowl. Combine vinegar and oil in a screw top jar. Use 1tbsp of herbs to 2 cups of lettuce leaves together with 15 ml (1tbsp) of dressing. Toss.

Makes 4 servings | Serving Size 102 g
Amount Per Serving | Calories 198 | Total Fat 21.5g | Cholesterol 0mg | Sodium 6mg | Potassium 152mg | Carbohydrates 3.0g | Sugars 0.7g | Protein 0.6g |

Good points | No cholesterol | Very low in sodium | Low in sugar | High in vitamin B6 |

Health Benefits Of Lettuce:
Contains vitamin C, beta-carotene, omega 3, protein. Helps with insomnia. Alkaline forming; helps remove toxins and keeps acid/alkaline in balance for more energy, clearer thinking and restful sleep.

Avocado Dressing

Per Serving: Sodium 3mg

Ingredients

3 tbsp lemon or lime juice

3 tbsp extra virgin olive oil

1/2 clove garlic

1 ripe avocado, peeled, mashed

2 tbsp white wine vinegar

Freshly ground black pepper

Method

Combine all ingredients in a bowl. Pour over fresh leafy salad greens.

Makes 8 servings | Serving Size 40 g

Amount Per Serving | Calories 99 | Total Fat 10.2g | Cholesterol 0mg | Sodium 3mg | Potassium 133mg | Carbohydrates 2.4g | Protein 0.5g |

Good points | **No cholesterol** | **Very low in sodium** | **Very low in sugar** |

Health Benefits Of Avocado:
Contains 25 essential nutrients and is considered one of the healthiest food on the planet. Vitamin A, B, C, E, iron, magnesium and potassium help protect the body.

Slow Roasted Tomatoes

Good with grilled meats, bread, soups.

Per Serving: Sodium 4mg

Ingredients

10 basil leaves

2 tbsp olive oil

6 tomatoes

Freshly ground black pepper

Method

Shred basil leaves and place in the oil. Leave to marinate for 1 hour. Wash tomatoes. Place on a baking tray. Drizzle with basil oil, grind black pepper over.

Bake in the middle of the oven. 160C (320F) 1 hour. Cool. Store in a jar in the fridge.

Makes 10 servings | Serving Size 77 g
Amount Per Serving | Calories 37 | Total Fat 2.9g | Cholesterol 0mg | Sodium 4mg | Potassium 177mg | Carbohydrates 2.9g | Sugars 1.9g | Protein 0.7g |

Good points | No cholesterol | Very low in sodium | High in iron | High in potassium | Very high in vitamin A | Very high in vitamin C |

Onion Jam

Per Serving: Sodium 2mg

Makes: 1 jar

Ingredients

6 large red onions, peeled, cut in rings
2 tbsp olive oil
2 tbsp brown sugar
1/2 cup water
1 tbsp balsamic vinegar
1 cup dry white wine or chicken stock
2 bay leaves
2 cloves
1 clove garlic, crushed
Freshly ground black pepper

Method

Heat oil in a frying pan. Add onions. Cook on medium heat until soft. Add sugar and 1/2 cup water. Cook 20 minutes until golden, stirring constantly to prevent onions catching on the bottom of pan. Add vinegar, stock or wine, bay leaves and cloves. Cook over low heat, stirring often. Cook 15 minutes until it looks like glossy jam. Cool. Store covered in the fridge for up to 1 week. Serve with grilled chicken, lamb, and beef.

Makes 14 servings | Serving Size 94 g
Amount Per Serving | Calories 64 | Total Fat 2.0g | Cholesterol 0mg | Sodium 2mg | Potassium 114mg | Carbohydrates 7.8g | Sugars 4.1g | Protein 0.5g |

Good points | No cholesterol | Very low in sodium | Very high in vitamin B6 | Very high in vitamin C |

Health Benefits Of Red onions:
Contains magnesium, potassium, manganese and vitamins C, K and B6. The outer layers of the skin contain concentrated vitamins, so peel as little of the outer layers as you can to get the most benefits.

Avocado Salsa

Per Serving: Sodium 5mg

Ingredients

3 tomatoes, seeded, diced
1 small red onion, finely chopped
1/3 cup coriander leaves, chopped
2 cloves garlic, crushed
3 tbsp light olive oil
Freshly ground black pepper
2 ripe avocado, peeled
1 lime, juiced

Method

Mix tomatoes, onion, coriander leaves and garlic in a bowl. Season with freshly ground black pepper to taste. Mash avocadoes with a fork. Stir into the salsa. Add lime juice. Store and serve with toasted pita bread or unsalted corn chips.

Makes 10 servings | Serving Size 90 g
Amount Per Serving | Calories 129 | Total Fat 12.1g | Cholesterol 0mg | Sodium 5mg | Potassium 298mg | Carbohydrates 5.8g | Sugars 1.5g | Protein 1.2g |

Good points | No cholesterol | Very low in sodium | High in dietary fiber | Very high in vitamin B6 | High in vitamin C |

Health Benefits Of Limes:
High in vitamin C, iron and minerals. Rich in flavonoids known for their antioxidant and antibiotic properties. Strengthens the immune system.

Orange Salad

Per Serving: Sodium 3mg

Ingredients

1 bunch rocket leaves
1 red onion, sliced thinly in rounds
2 oranges, peeled, round slices, (save the juice)
3 tbsp pine nuts, pecans, or walnut pieces

Method

Lightly toasted nuts in a frying pan. Place rocket on a serving plate. Place slices of oranges and onion on top of the rocket leaves. Sprinkle with toasted nuts. Drizzle with orange juice.

Makes 4 servings | Serving Size 136 g

Amount Per Serving | Calories 101 | Total Fat 4.6g | Cholesterol 0mg | Sodium 3mg | Potassium 282mg | Carbohydrates 14.6g | Sugars 10.2g | Protein 2.2g |

Good points | Low in saturated fat | No cholesterol | Very low in sodium | High in dietary fiber | Very high in manganese | Very high in vitamin B6 | Very high in vitamin C |

Avocado And Citrus Salad

Per Serving: Sodium 8mg

Ingredients

2 avocados, peeled and sliced

2 oranges, peeled and sectioned

1 small bunch mint leaves

Poppy seed dressing:

1 lemon, juiced

4 tbsp olive oil

1 1/2 tbsp poppy seeds (make sure they are fresh)

Method

Cut avocado into chunks. Cut oranges into chunks.

Arrange salad greens on a plate. Top with oranges and avocado. Combine poppy seed dressing ingredients together in a screw top jar. Shake well. Add a grind of black pepper. Shake. Pour over the salad and serve. Garnish with mint leaves.

Makes 4 servings | Serving Size 214 g
Amount Per Serving | Calories 387 | Total Fat 35.2g | Cholesterol 0mg | Sodium 8mg | Potassium 690mg | Carbohydrates 20.5g | Sugars 9.5g | Protein 3.5g |

Good points | No cholesterol | Very low in sodium | Very high in vitamin C |

Marinated Bean Salad

Per Serving: Sodium 25mg

Ingredients

2 cups cooked green beans

1 green capsicum, chopped

1 small red onion, grated

1 cup celery, sliced

Dressing:

1/2 tsp white pepper

3 tbsp sugar

6 tbsp white wine vinegar

12 tbsp extra virgin olive oil

1/4 cup water

Method

Combine vegetables in a bowl. Combine salad ingredients in a screw top jar. Shake well. Pour over the vegetables. Cover and refrigerate for 1 day.

Makes 4 servings | Serving Size 189 g
Amount Per Serving | Calories 428 | Total Fat 42.1g | Cholesterol 0mg | Sodium 25mg | Potassium 226mg | Carbohydrates 15.7g | Sugars 10.9g | Protein 1.3g |

Good points | No cholesterol | Very low in sodium | Very high in vitamin B6 |

Health Benefits Of White Wine Vinegar:
Protects against heart disease and cancer and may help slow the aging process. Vinegar acts as a substitute for salt in a low sodium diet.

Mediterranean Vegetables

This is great with lamb and fish. If you have a big enough oven dish, it's easy to double this recipe for a crowd.

Per Serving: Sodium 16mg

Ingredients

400g fresh Italian tomatoes, chopped
3 medium red onions, peeled and quartered
2 red capsicum, deseeded, cut in thick strips
1 yellow capsicum, deseeded, cut in thick strips
8 small potatoes, skin on, parboiled 10 minutes
2 cloves garlic, chopped
Big handful roughly chopped oregano
3 tbsp olive oil

Freshly ground black pepper
Fresh basil leaves, shredded

Method

Heat oven to 200 C. Toss vegetables except tomatoes in oil. Place in a baking tray and cook for 20 minutes. Remove from oven and add tomatoes. Toss. Return to oven and cook for a further 15 minutes. Remove from oven. Add freshly ground pepper and torn basil leaves.

Makes 8 servings | Serving Size 294 g
Amount Per Serving | Calories 225 | Total Fat 6.5g
Cholesterol 0mg | Sodium 16mg | Potassium 1080mg | Carbohydrates 40.1g | Sugars 6.3g | Protein 5.0g |

Good points | No cholesterol | Very low in sodium | High in dietary fiber | High in iron | High in manganese | High in potassium | High in vitamin A | Very high in vitamin B6 | Very high in vitamin C |

Health Benefits Of Red Potatoes:
Packed with starch for concentrated energy. High in essential iron and vitamin C, zinc and copper for a healthy nervous system.

Tomato And Mint Salad

Per Serving: Sodium 11mg

Ingredients

500g ripe acid-free Italian tomatoes, sliced

Juice 1 lemon

Freshly ground black pepper

1/4 tsp caster sugar

Small bunch fresh mint leaves, washed

1/2 tsp grated lemon zest

Cos lettuce leaves

Method

Marinate tomatoes in lemon juice, black pepper; caster sugar, lemon zest and shredded mint leaves for 30 minutes. Place two spoonfuls in a fresh cos lettuce leaf 'plate'. Serve on a platter as a salad or to accompany hot or cold meat.

Makes 4 servings | Serving Size 200 g
Amount Per Serving | Calories 37 | Cholesterol 0mg | Sodium 11mg | Potassium 419mg | Carbohydrates 8.5g | Sugars 4.4g | Protein 1.7g |

Good points | Low in saturated fat | No cholesterol | Low in sodium | Very high in dietary fiber | Very high in iron | Very high in manganese | High in magnesium | High in niacin | High in phosphorus | Very high in potassium | High in thiamin | Very high in vitamin A | Very high in vitamin B6 |

Health Benefits Of Cos Lettuce:

Heart healthy with high levels of vitamin C and K. Contains potassium, fiber and folate.

Roasted Red Peppers

Per Serving: Sodium 10mg

Ingredients

6 red or yellow capsicums
3 tbsp extra virgin olive oil
Freshly ground black pepper
2 tbsp fresh basil, chopped
Freshly ground black pepper

Method

Heat oven to 190 C. Place peppers in an oven dish and drizzle with a little olive oil. Place in the oven and grill until tender, turning until the skin is blackened and blistered. Remove from oven and seal in a plastic bag. Leave for 10 minutes. Place on a cutting board. Peel the skin off the peppers. Holding over a bowl to save the juice, cut the capsicums in half and remove the seeds. Discard seeds but keep the juice. Cut into long strips. Mix remaining ingredients in a small bowl. Add capsicum juice. Arrange on a plate and spoon dressing over. Serve at room temperature.

Makes 4 servings | Serving Size 251 g
Amount Per Serving | Calories 164 | Total Fat 11.2g | Cholesterol 0mg | Sodium 10mg | Potassium 506mg | Carbohydrates 14.4g | Sugars 10.0g | Protein 2.4g |

Good points | No cholesterol | Very low in sodium | High in dietary fiber | Very high in vitamin A | Very high in vitamin B6 | Very high in vitamin C |

Zucchini Fritters

Per Serving: Sodium 41mg

Ingredients

1 zucchini

1 large egg

3 tbsp plain flour

1/2 tsp baking powder

1 tbsp onion, finely chopped

1 clove garlic, crushed

1 tbsp fresh mint leaves, finely chopped

1 tsp lemon or lime juice

freshly ground black pepper

1 tsp melted unsalted butter

Extra unsalted butter for frying

Method

Grate zucchini. Squeeze juice out with your hands and discard. Place zucchini in a kitchen towel. Squeeze out any remaining juice (you can save juice and use in soup stocks).

Place egg and flour in a bowl. Mix until smooth. Add zucchini, onion, garlic, mint, lemon juice, melted butter and pepper. Mix well.

Melt butter in a heavy based frying pan. Spoon mixture into hot pan. Cook for 3 minutes each side until browned and cooked through. Serve with fresh tomato salsa. You can replace zucchini with sweetcorn (cut kernels from 3 fresh cobs) and use coriander leaves instead of mint.

Makes 4 servings | Serving Size 173 g
Amount Per Serving | Calories 75 | Cholesterol 49mg | Sodium 41mg | Potassium 487mg | Carbohydrates 10.4g | Sugars 2.8g | Protein 4.1g |

Good points | High in dietary fiber | High in manganese | High in phosphorus | High in potassium | High in riboflavin | High in selenium | High in thiamin | High in vitamin A | Very high in vitamin B6 | Very high in vitamin C |

Spinach Tart

Per Serving: Sodium 111mg

Makes 2 26-28 cm tarts

Ingredients

1 cup (250g) low salt cream cheese or homemade ricotta or mascarpone

6 eggs

1 cup milk

2 tbsp basil leaves

2 spring onions, pale part only, chopped

500g baby spinach leaves

1/4 tsp nutmeg, freshly grated

Freshly ground black pepper

Ingredients For Pastry

2 cups flour

150g unsalted butter

About 4 tbsp cold water

Method

Heat oven to 200 C. Grease two 26-28 cm quiche or flan baking dishes.

Make Pastry: Place flour and butter in a food processor. Process until fine breadcrumbs. Slowly drizzle in enough water to make pastry hold together in a soft ball. Roll or press pastry into the dishes. Blind bake, part cooking pastry until golden brown, about 10-12 minutes. Remove from oven and cool.

While pastry is baking, blend spinach, cream cheese, eggs, milk and basil leaves together. Add pepper and nutmeg to make a smooth green puree. Reduce oven to 180 C. Pour puree into pastry casings. Bake for 30 minutes until filling is set in the center. You can test this with a clean knife. Serve warm or hot. You can freeze the quiches. To reheat from frozen, remove from freezer for 1 hour. Bake at 180 C for 15-20 minutes until heated through. Serve with tomato salsa.

Makes 8 servings | Serving Size 162 g
Amount Per Serving | Calories 79 | Total Fat 4.2g | Cholesterol 125mg | Sodium 111mg | Potassium 423mg | Carbohydrates 4.4g | Sugars 2.0g | Protein 7.0g |

Good points | High in calcium | High in iron | Very high in manganese | High in magnesium | High in phosphorus | High in potassium | High in riboflavin | Very high in selenium | Very high in vitamin A | Very high in vitamin B6 | High in vitamin B12 | Very high in vitamin C |

Health Benefits Of Nutmeg:
Good for anxiety and depression. Fights fatigue and stress.

Bus Stop Potatoes

Per Serving: Sodium 17mg

Ingredients

16 small round potatoes, washed

1 tbsp extra virgin olive oil

1 tbsp fennel, cumin, or caraway seeds

1 tbsp fresh chopped rosemary or thyme

Method

Preheat oven to 250 C. Leave skins on potatoes. Place in a saucepan of water and bring to boil. Simmer for 10 minutes until not quite cooked. Drain. Transfer to a lightly greased baking tray. Squash each potato flat with a potato masher, so they look like they have been run over by a bus! Brush the top of each with oil and scatter cumin seeds, or caraway seeds and black pepper. Bake on top shelf of oven for 20-25 minutes until crisp and golden.

Makes 10 servings | Serving Size 274 g
Amount Per Serving | Calories 201 | Total Fat 1.7g | Cholesterol 0mg | Sodium 17mg | Potassium 1112mg | Carbohydrates 43.0g | Sugars 3.1g | Protein 4.6g |

Good points | Very low in saturated fat | No cholesterol | Very low in sodium | High in dietary fiber | High in potassium | High in vitamin B6 | Very high in vitamin C |

Irish Potato Cake

Per Serving: Sodium 65mg

Ingredients

6 large potatoes

Freshly ground black pepper

1 tsp thyme leaves

3 tbsp unsalted butter, melted

Method

Peel potatoes and cut in thin slices. Butter a 20cm flan ring and place on a buttered baking sheet. Arrange the potato slices in the ring in layers. Sprinkle with thyme and pepper between each layer. Pour melted butter over the top layer. Bake in a 190 C oven for 45 minutes or until golden brown. To serve, loosen the edges of the potato cake, by running a knife around the inside of the tin. Remove ring. Cut into sections and serve.

Makes 5 servings | Serving Size 264 g
Amount Per Serving | Calories 238 | Total Fat 7.2g | Cholesterol 18mg | Sodium 65mg | Potassium 1044mg | Carbohydrates 40.3g | Sugars 2.9g | Protein 4.4g |

Good points | Low in sodium | High in potassium | High in vitamin B6 | Very high in vitamin C |

Health Benefits Of Unsalted Butter:
Rich in vitamin A (necessary for adrenal health). Great source of vitamins E, K and D. Protects against calcification of joints and hardening of the arteries. Provides a quick source of energy.

Hot Potato Wedges

These potato wedges are fluffy inside yet browned and crisp outside.

Per Serving: Sodium 10mg

Ingredients

1 kg of potatoes, unpeeled, washed
1/4 cup (60ml) olive oil

Method

Heat oven to 200 C (180 C fan-bake)
Oil two oven trays. Cut potatoes into wedge shapes. Place in a large bowl. Add olive oil and toss. Place on single layers on baking trays. Brush with spice mixture of your choice. Roast

uncovered, turning occasionally, for 30-40 minutes until crisp, lightly browned and cooked through.

SPICES FOR FLAVORING WEDGES

Lemon Pepper:
Combine 1 tbsp each of finely grated lemon rind and lemon juice and 1 tsp of black pepper.

Cajun Pepper:
Combine 1/2 tsp ground oregano, 2 tsp ground cumin, 1 tsp smoky paprika, 1 tsp ground turmeric and 1 tsp ground coriander powder with 1/2 tsp black pepper in a small bowl.

Garlic And Lime:
Place 1 1/2 tbsp oil, 5 garlic cloves (unpeeled and crushed) and 1 1/2 tbsp lime juice in a bowl. Whisk to combine. Add black pepper.

Makes 6 servings | Serving Size 177 g
Amount Per Serving | Calories 196 | Total Fat 9.6g | Cholesterol 0mg | Sodium 10mg | Potassium 678mg | Carbohydrates 26.2g | Sugars 1.9g | Protein 2.8g |

Good points | No cholesterol | Very low in sodium | Very high in vitamin C |

Roasted Beetroot Salad

Per Serving: Sodium 67mg

Ingredients

2 beetroot, cut in 2 cm cubes
1 large red onion, peeled cut in thick rounds
6 cloves garlic, sliced
2 tbsp extra virgin olive oil
3 tbsp roasted pine nuts
1 cup rocket leaves
80g homemade mozzarella

Dressing:

100g frozen raspberries, thawed
1/4 cup orange juice
1/4 cup balsamic vinegar

Method

Heat oven to 190 C. Toss beets, onion, garlic and oil in a roasting pan. Season and bake for 45-50 minutes. Cool. Place in a bowl and toss with pine nuts, rocket leaves and dressing. Serve with mozzarella and extra rocket leaves to garnish.

Make Dressing:

Place raspberries, orange juice and vinegar in a small pan. Bring to boil over medium heat. Place in a blender and blend until smooth. Cool and strain.

Makes 4 servings | Serving Size 249 g
Amount Per Serving | Calories 194
Total Fat 12.0g | Saturated Fat 1.4g | Cholesterol 0mg | Sodium 67mg | Potassium 436mg | Carbohydrates 18.4g | Sugars 10.8g | Protein 4.8g |

Good points | No cholesterol | Low in sodium | High in manganese | Very high in vitamin B6 | Very high in vitamin C |

Health Benefits Of Pine Nuts:
Rich in vitamin A. High in iron. Boosts energy levels.

Beetroot And Orange Salad

Per Serving: Sodium 118mg

Ingredients

12 baby beetroot with leaves
1/2 cup balsamic vinegar
2 oranges, juiced
Rind of two oranges cut in fine julienned strips
100g walnuts or pine nuts, roasted
2 tbsp finely chopped chives

Method

Cut leaves from beets. Wash and drain. Wash beets. Place on a baking tray with 2 cups of water. Cover with foil and bake at 190 C for 45 minutes or until tender. Drain. Cool slightly, then peel. Cut warm beets into wedges and combine with balsamic and pepper to taste in a shallow heatproof bowl. Place in a turned off oven for 1 hour. Turn the oven on low to reheat the beets just before serving. Combine remaining ingredients, except walnuts and chives, in a saucepan and stir until warm. Tear larger beet leaves into pieces and arrange with small beet leaves on a serving plate. Top with beets and drizzle with warm dressing. Sprinkle with walnuts and chives. Serve.

Makes 4 servings | Serving Size 299 g
Amount Per Serving | Calories 270 | Total Fat 15.1g | Saturated Fat 0.9g | Cholesterol 0mg | Sodium 118mg | Potassium 781mg | Carbohydrates 28.6g | Sugars 21.0g | Protein 9.4g |

Good points | Low in saturated fat | No cholesterol | Low in sodium | High in dietary fiber | High in manganese | Very high in vitamin C |

Health Benefits Of Balsamic Vinegar:
Keeps blood glucose levels steady. Normalizes blood pressure.

Best Potato Salad Ever

This is a bit of a family secret and comes from a hand written note to my sister, from a head chef in a local café she frequented in the 1960's.

Per Serving: Sodium 16mg

Ingredients

5 medium potatoes, peeled, diced

1 small red onion, finely diced

1 handful mint leaves, finely chopped

1 tbsp extra virgin olive oil

1 tsp white wine vinegar

1/4 cup toasted unsalted cashew nuts

Method

Cook potatoes until tender. Drain. Place in a bowl. Add mint, onion and freshly ground black pepper to taste. Add olive oil. Toss carefully. Add vinegar. Season to taste. Add more or less vinegar and oil to suit your palate. Chill in the fridge.

Makes 5 servings | Serving Size 240 g
Amount Per Serving | Calories 181 | Total Fat 3.1g | Cholesterol 0mg | Sodium 16mg | Potassium 930mg | Carbohydrates 35.5g | Sugars 3.1g | Protein 4.0g |

Good points | Low in saturated fat | No cholesterol | Very low in sodium | High in dietary fiber | High in potassium | Very high in vitamin B6 | Very high in vitamin C |

Pumpkin Salad

Per Serving: Sodium 8mg

Ingredients

500g pumpkin, peeled and cut in 2 cm cubes

1/2 tsp cumin seeds

3 cloves garlic, unpeeled

Freshly ground black pepper

2 tbsp extra virgin olive oil

1 bunch water cress, or mixed lettuce leaves

1 small red onion, thinly sliced

Lemon dressing:

1 tbsp lemon juice

2 tbsp extra virgin olive oil

1 tbsp honey, or fruit jam

Freshly ground black pepper

Method

Heat oven to 190 C. Toss pumpkin, cumin, garlic, and pepper with 2 tbsp olive oil. Place in a roasting tray and cook for 20-30 minutes until pumpkin is cooked, but still firm. Combine dressing ingredients together in a screw top jar. Place onions and baby lettuce in a bowl. Add warm cooked pumpkin. Add dressing and toss ingredients until combined.

Makes 4 servings | Serving Size 172 g
Amount Per Serving | Calories 192 | Total Fat 14.5g | Saturated Fat 2.2g | Cholesterol 0mg | Sodium 8mg | Potassium 312mg | Carbohydrates 17.1g | Sugars 9.3g | Protein 1.8g |

Good points | No cholesterol | Very low in sodium | Very high in vitamin A | Very high in vitamin B6 |

Roasted Eggplant Salad

Per Serving: Sodium 12mg

Ingredients

1 eggplant, sliced

3 baby beetroot, cut in 4 pieces

1 red capsicum, cut in 4 pieces

1 yellow capsicum, cut in 4 pieces

1 yellow zucchini, sliced

1 green zucchini, sliced

1 red onion, cut in 4

Fresh rosemary leaves

Fresh sage leaves (or use basil, oregano)

1 clove garlic, crushed
Extra virgin olive oil
1 tbsp balsamic vinegar
Black pepper

Method

Mix garlic with olive oil and season with freshly ground black pepper.

Place vegetables in a large baking tray. Spread them out and brush with garlic oil. Place under a medium hot grill. Grill until the skins begin to blister and darken. Remove from oven and toss balsamic through the vegetables. Place on a serving platter. Drizzle with a little olive oil and place fresh sprigs of herbs through the warm vegetables for garnish.

You can vary the vegetables and use whatever you have in your fridge: very thin slices of pumpkin, sweet potatoes, parsnips, carrots (cut lengthways), tomatoes cut in half, whole shallots, spring onions. Instead of grilling, you can bake the vegetables. Add rosemary and garlic to the oven tray. Then bake at 190 C for 20-30 minutes.

Makes 5 servings | Serving Size 267 g
Amount Per Serving | Calories 115 | Total Fat 3.4g | Cholesterol 0mg | Sodium 12mg | Potassium 563mg | Carbohydrates 15.0g | Sugars 7.1g | Protein 2.9g |

Good points | No cholesterol | Very low in sodium | High in manganese | High in potassium | Very high in vitamin A | Very high in vitamin B6 | Very high in vitamin C |

Health Benefits Eggplant:
Vitamin A, C, E and K, copper, iron, zinc, magnesium.

Lemon Garlic Mushrooms

Per Serving: Sodium 36mg

Ingredients

50g unsalted butter

2 cloves garlic, crushed

1 tsp fresh thyme

1 tbsp lemon juice

12 flat mushrooms, stalks removed

Olive oil

Method

Place butter in a saucepan with garlic cloves and thyme. Heat on medium heat until butter melts and garlic is transparent. Take care not to brown. Remove from heat. Add lemon juice. Butter an oven dish. Place mushroom skin side up and brush with garlic butter. Grill for two minutes. Turn over. Brush with remainder of garlic butter until cooked. Serve on toasted bread or as a side dish to accompany red meat or chicken.

Makes 4 servings | Serving Size 127 g
Amount Per Serving | Calories 152 | Total Fat 14.9g | Cholesterol 11mg | Sodium 36mg | Potassium 348mg | Carbohydrates 4.2g | Sugars 1.9g | Protein 3.5g |

Good points | Low in sodium | High in iron | High in niacin | High in pantothenic acid | High in riboflavin | High in selenium | Very high in vitamin B6 |

Mint Orzo Salad

Per Serving: Sodium 30mg

Ingredients

200g orzo

1/4 cup raisins or currants

1/4 cup pine nuts

1/2 cup parsley, chopped

1/2 cup mint, chopped

1 red capsicum, diced

1/2 cup celery, chopped

Dressing

2 tbsp olive oil mustard

1 tbsp white wine vinegar

2 tbsp pomegranate molasses

2 tbsp orange juice

1/2 tsp curry powder

1/2 tsp ground cumin seeds

1 tsp whole grain mustard

Method

Place grain mustard, curry powder and cumin powder in a screw top jar. Add the rest of the dressing ingredients and mix well. Leave for 30 minutes for the raisins to plump. Cook orzo in boiling water for 7-10 minutes until al dente. Drain well. Place in a bowl. Add pine nuts, parsley, mint, capsicum and celery. Add salad dressing. Toss.

Makes 4 servings | Serving Size 160 g
Amount Per Serving | Calories 384 | Total Fat 14.2g | Cholesterol 0mg | Sodium 30mg | Potassium 481mg | Carbohydrates 57.6g | Sugars 16.0g | Protein 8.7g |

Good points | Low in saturated fat | No cholesterol | Very low in sodium | High in vitamin A | Very high in vitamin C |

Evergreen Café's Hummus Salad

Per Serving: Sodium 23mg

Ingredients

2 cups chickpeas, soaked overnight

3 tbsp lemon juice

3 tbsp homemade tahini no salt added (ground sesame) paste

2 cloves garlic, crushed

1/2 tsp cumin seeds, ground

2 tbsp, low-acid extra virgin olive oil

Freshly ground black pepper

3 ripe tomatoes, chopped

1 cucumber, peeled and chopped

1 tbsp red wine vinegar

2 tbsp olive oil (for dressing)

1 tbsp flat leaf parsley, for garnish

Method

Drain soaked chickpeas. Place in saucepan. Bring to boil. Reduce heat and simmer until tender, about 30 minutes to 1 hour.

Drain peas and place in food processor or blender. Add lemon juice, tahini, oil, cumin, olive oil and pepper. Blend until smooth. Taste and adjust seasoning. Add more lemon juice, pepper or cumin to taste.

Place chopped tomatoes, cucumber, oil, vinegar and pepper in a bowl. Mix well.

Place hummus in a shallow serving dish. Spoon cucumber and tomatoes salad over the hummus. Serve at room temperature with bread for dipping.

Makes 6 servings | Serving Size 200 g
Amount Per Serving | Calories 332 | Total Fat 11.2g | Cholesterol 0mg | Sodium 23mg | Potassium 846mg | Carbohydrates 46.4g | Sugars 9.8g | Protein 14.7g

Good points | No cholesterol | Very low in sodium | High in dietary fiber | High in iron | High in manganese

Tabbouleh Salad

Per Serving: Sodium 18mg

155g burghul cracked wheat
1/2 cup spring onion, finely diced
3 tbsp lemon juice
2 tbsp light virgin olive oil
1 cup flat-leaf parsley, chopped
2 tbsp mint, finely chopped
375g ripe tomatoes, peeled, finely diced

Method

Soak cracked wheat in cold water for 1 hour. Drain and squeeze all the water out. Combine with lemon juice, oil and pepper. Add spring onion, mint leaves and parsley. Season with pepper. Serve.

Makes 4 servings | Serving Size 182 g
Amount Per Serving | Calories 193
Total Fat 7.9g | Saturated Fat 1.2g | Cholesterol 0mg | Sodium 18mg | Potassium 367mg | Carbohydrates 27.9g | Sugars 3.1g | Protein 4.5g |

Good points | No cholesterol | Very low in sodium | High in dietary fiber | High in iron | Very high in vitamin A | Very high in vitamin C |

Health Benefits Of Bulgur wheat:
Impressive amounts of manganese helps protect the body from free radicals.

MEASUREMENTS

Liquid Measures

1 tsp	=	5 mls
1 tbsb	=	20 mls
4 cups	=	1 liter
1/2 cup	=	125 mls

Solid measures

32 oz	=	1 kilogram
16 oz	=	500 grams
8oz	=	250 grams
7oz	=	220 grams
6 oz	=	185 grams
5 oz	=	155 grams
4 oz	=	125 grams
3 oz	=	90 grams
2 oz	=	60 grams
1 oz	=	30 grams

Oven Temperatures

Degree F		Degree C
200	=	100
225	=	110
250	=	120
275	=	140
300	=	150
325	=	160
350	=	180
375	=	190
400	=	200
425	=	220
450	=	230
475	=	240

Glossary

Al Dente: Cooked until tender but firm to the bite. A term used to describe perfectly cooked pasta.

Baking Soda: Bicarbonate of soda, raising agent. Substitute regular baking soda for sodium-free baking soda. Low sodium content baking soda is available in supermarkets, specialty food stores and health food stores.

Baking Powder: Most commercial baking powders contain sodium aluminum sulphate, although brands such as Haine Featherweight Baking Powder *contain 0 mg per 1/4 teaspoon.*

You can make a baking powder substitute at home by mixing 1/2 teaspoon cream of tartar with 1/4 teaspoon of low sodium baking soda. Use to replace 1 teaspoon of baking powder in recipes. There is a site selling sodium-free and low sodium products online at healthyheartmarket.com.

Beetroots: Beets.

Balsamic Vinegar: A superior vinegar using a centuries old Italian technique. Aromatic, spicy and sweet sour taste.

Borlotti Beans: Small, speckled beans that are pale pinkish in color.

Bulgur Wheat: Dried cracked wheat.

Buttermilk: Makes baking lighter. You can make you own version simply by mixing 1 cup of milk and 1 tbsp of lemon juice.

Cake Tin: Cake/baking pan.

Chickpeas: Garbanzo beans.

Citrus Zest: The finely grated rind of citrus fruit. 1 lime = 1 tsp (teaspoon) of grated zest; 1 lemon = 2 tsp zest; I orange = 1 tbsp (tablespoon) zest; the juice of 1 lime = about 2 tbsp and the juice of 1 lemon = 4 tbsp or 1/4 cup.

Cos Lettuce: Romaine lettuce.

Coriander: Cilantro.

Cornflour: Cornstarch.

Creme Fraiche: Similar in flavor to sour cream. Used in both sweet and savory dishes.

Essence: Extract.

Eggplant: Aubergine.

Flour: Plain = standard flour.

Frying Pan: Skillet/frypan.

Ginger: 2 cm ginger root = 1 tsp finely grated ginger or 1 tbsp roughly grated.

Green Prawns: Raw prawns. Keep a bag in the freezer for quick meals.

Grill: Broil. To cook under the top oven element, or on the barbecue grill.

Hard-boiled Egg: Hard-cooked egg.

Icing Sugar: Confectioners sugar.

Kaffir Lime Leaves: Dark green glossy leaves add a citrus flavor. Shred and add to Asian style dishes.

King Prawns: Jumbo shrimp/scampi.

Lemongrass: A thick stalk with fragrant flavor. Easily found in most supermarkets. Be sure to peel away the tough outer layers of the stalk and use the tender parts.

Mascarpone: A fresh Italian cream cheese that can be used in both sweet and savory dishes. Follow the recipe in the book to save money and make your own salt free version at home.

Minced Meat: Ground meat

Mozzarella: Italian style cheese. See the recipe in this book and make your own at home.

Oven Temperatures: Oven temperatures vary

depending if your oven is fan baked or not. Use cooking times as a guide. Check oven-baked dishes during cooking when trying a recipe for the first time. Always preheat your oven to start.

Passata: A brand name for tomatoes that have been skinned, deseeded and pulped. Usually sold in tall glass jars. It is the same type of puree you get if you mash canned tomatoes with a fork.

Pine Nuts: Seeds of the stone pine. Small, nutty and creamy tasting. Buy in small quantities and keep in the fridge to prevent them going rancid.

Polenta: Corn maize from Italy. Rich and golden in color. Milder than cornmeal with a smooth texture. Red kidney beans can be used instead. Soak all dried beans overnight before cooking.

Pomegranate Molasses: Specialty ingredient from delicatessens and supermarkets.

Ricotta Cheese: Soft curd, low fat cheese. Use in savory and sweet dishes. Make your own ricotta by using the recipe in this book.

Rocket: Arugula, rocquette, rucola, rugula.

Roma Or Plum Tomatoes: Egg-shaped tomatoes with plenty of juicy flesh and a few seeds. Ideal for making sauces. My preference is for Italian style Roma tomatoes as they are less acidic. Add a pinch of sugar where tomatoes are acid. Always chose robust, flavorsome, ripe and red. A truss of organic tomatoes, fully ripened gives more obvious flavor to food than pale force ripened ones.

Seed: Pip.

Shallots: Small sized onions with a sweeter taste than regular onions. Delicious whole or roasted. can be chopped and added to sauces and salsas.

Simmer: To cook just under bpoiling point- small bubbles may erupt in one place.

Smokey Paprika: A spice made from ground capsicums(bell peppers). Adds a smoky flavor and to barbequed, grilled or roasted meat, chicken and vegetables. The Spanish paprika is the smoked variety called *Pimenton* and is available in sweet *(dulce)*, moderate or sweet and sour *(agridulce)* and spicy *(picante)*.

Spring Onions: Green onions or scallions.

Steam: To cook food in a rising steam.

Stock: Enriched 'cooking water' produced from simmering stock ingredients. Using homemade no salt stock from fresh ingredients makes all the difference to your cooking.

Sweet Peppers: Capsicum/bell peppers.

Thai Basil: A stronger, peppery flavor compared to

Italian basil. Used in Asian style dishes.

Tomato Products: Canned Italian tomatoes are a superior product, rich, sweet and full of flavor. Buy reduced sodium or no salt cans.

Turmeric: An aromatic spice from the same family as the ginger root plant, so you can use it in the same way. Adds color and warm peppery flavor.

Vanilla: Use natural vanilla extract where possible. Use vanilla bean pods when heating milk. Scrape out the seeds and use with flavored milk for custards and desserts. Keep a pod in a jar of sugar to make vanilla sugar for baking and desserts.

Vermicelli Noodles: Thin noodles made from rice. Hydrate in water before you use. Add to salads and stir fries.

SALTLESS BOOKS

www.ingramcontent.com/pod-product-compliance
Lightning Source LLC
Chambersburg PA
CBHW061944070426
42450CB00007BA/1049